CONTENTS

CHAPTER 1

THE PATH TO WAR

The Great War was a military conflict waiting to happen. In 1870–1871, war between two of the world's major powers had resulted in a change in the balance of power in Europe. The Germans, led by the king of Prussia, had defeated France and annexed the French provinces of Alsace and Lorraine. As a result, the powerful German Empire was created and the Prussian king was made its emperor, or kaiser. Following its defeat in 1871, France sought to regain control of Alsace-Lorraine and became fearful of Germany's increased fighting power. The Russian Empire was also unhappy with Germany's growing military strength and had ongoing conflicts with Germany's ally, the Habsburg-ruled Austro-Hungarian Empire. In January 1894, the French Republic formed the Franco-Russian Alliance with the Russian Empire against their joint enemy.

The tension between the Franco-Russian alliance and the Central Powers, Germany and Austria–Hungary, grew over the next 40 years. During this period of peace, the major powers of Europe – Britain, Germany, France, Austria-Hungary and Russia – all competed to build bigger armies and better armaments than their rivals. On the European mainland, compulsory military service for men was imposed by many governments, and countries were prepared to mobilize armies of millions of men in a matter of days.

The mighty British battleship HMS *Dreadnought* was launched in 1906. The building of *Dreadnought*, and other battleships of its class, was part of a naval arms race between Britain and Germany.

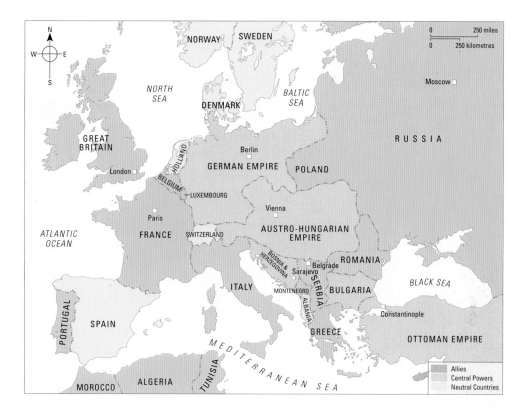

A dangerous arms race

In 1899, Tsar Nicholas II, the ruler of Russia, warned that the arms race in Europe – the constant struggle to produce larger armies, heavier guns and bigger warships – would one day lead to war instead of preserving peace:

'The accelerating arms race is transforming the armed peace into a crushing burden that weighs on all nations, and if prolonged, will lead to the very cataclysm it seeks to avert.'

John Keegan, *The First World War* (Hutchinson, 1998)

Before the war, the major conflicts in Europe were between the Central Powers – the German and Austro–Hungarian Empires – and France and the Russian Empire. After war was declared, Britain joined the side of France and Russia.

Britain did not join the European alliances because the British government hoped its powerful navy would keep it safe from any invasion. However, at the beginning of the 20th century, the British became increasingly worried about the rising power of Germany. In 1900, the Germans began to build new warships that would challenge Britain's supremacy at sea. The British responded by building bigger and more powerful ships – a naval arms race was underway. In 1904, Britain negotiated an entente cordiale with France. This was an informal agreement on issues that

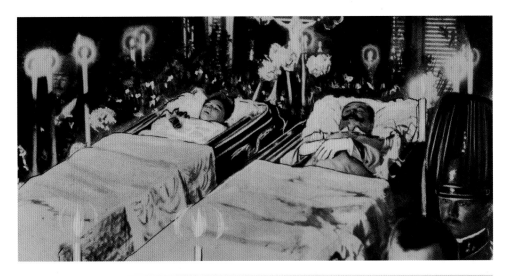

The assassination of Archduke Franz Ferdinand and his wife gave the Austro-Hungarian government an excuse to declare war on Serbia. Their bodies lay in state before they were buried.

might cause tension between France and Britain and Germany. British and French military leaders began working together on plans to defend their countries if there was a German attack.

At the turn of the 20th century, both Britain and France ruled large colonial empires in Africa and Asia. Germany, however, despite its strong economy and military resources, had only a small overseas empire. The Germans were unhappy about this and actively sought to increase their influence outside Europe. This directly threatened British and French interests. For example, in 1905, and again in 1911, Germany challenged France's influence in Morocco in a deliberate attempt to provoke a situation that would weaken and test the alliance between Britain and France. These confrontations were ultimately settled by diplomatic talks and compromise, but in 1911 in particular, they strengthened Britain

and France's relationship and brought Europe to the very brink of war.

In 1913, France reacted to these threats from Germany by introducing radical plans to expand the size of its conscript army. Russia was also growing in military strength to keep up with the other European powers. The German leaders complained of 'encirclement' by Russia and France. To them, it seemed that Germany was surrounded by potential enemies.

ON THE EDGE OF WAR

The situation reached crisis point in the Balkans. Two wars involving Balkan states and the Ottoman Empire were fought in 1912–1913. These conflicts resulted in a great increase in the power and territory of Serbia. As Slavs, the Serbs were supported by Russia, the leading Slav power. But the growth in Slav strength was very worrying to Austria–Hungary, which

The archduke's death

The date of 28 June 1914 was to be the turning point in the increasing tensions between rival nations in Europe. Archduke Franz Ferdinand, heir to the throne of Austria–Hungary, visited Sarajevo, in the province of Bosnia. Among the crowds gathered to see the archduke was 19-year-old Gavrilo Princip and five other young Bosnians who planned to assassinate the archduke. They wanted to free Bosnia from Austro–Hungarian rule and make it part of Serbia. Their first attempt to kill the archduke with a bomb failed. But later the same day, the archduke's car stopped near a shop where Gavrilo Princip had gone to buy a sandwich. He pulled out a gun and shot the archduke and his wife. Their deaths were the spark that ignited World War I.

had a substantial Slav minority among its multinational population, and which in 1908 had annexed Bosnia and Herzegovina, two provinces with a large Serb population.

Then, in 1914, an event took place that would drive much of Europe into one of the most appalling wars ever fought. The Austrian archduke Franz Ferdinand – heir to the Austro-Hungarian throne – was shot by a Serb nationalist during a visit to Bosnia on 28 June. All the top Austro-Hungarian military and political leaders rushed to make the assassination the reason for declaring war on Serbia. They wanted a military victory that would strengthen the Habsburg empire and put the upstart Slav state in its place. The Austrian emperor, Franz Josef, was more cautious and insisted on consulting his German allies. The German emperor, Kaiser Wilhelm II, assured Austria-Hungary that it could 'rely on Germany's full support'.

Tsar Nicholas II of Russia (left) and Germany's Kaiser Wilhelm II (right) ride side by side in a royal carriage about two years before the war. All the royal heads of state in Europe were closely related, but with the start of the conflict, they would become enemies.

Europe's leaders were slow to fully appreciate the seriousness of the situation. It was not until almost a month after the assassination, on 23 July, that the Austro-Hungarian government sent an ultimatum to the Serbian government, threatening to declare war unless a series of humiliating demands were met. The Serbs agreed to most of the demands, but not all. Austria-Hungary saw its opportunity and, on 28 July, declared war on Serbia.

The Austro-Hungarian declaration of war led with breathtaking speed to a general European war. The war plans of all countries included moving huge numbers of troops as quickly as possible by train. All countries feared a surprise attack from the enemy before all their forces were in place. Germany felt itself in an especially difficult situation because it expected to have to fight a war on two fronts – against Russia in the east and France in the west. Germany's war plan, the Schlieffen Plan, was based on gaining a rapid victory

Thousands of volunteers to join the British army are escorted through the streets by soldiers. In the autumn of 1914, the British army received about 30,000 new recruits every day.

VOICES FROM HISTORY

Leaving for war

A British soldier described the mixed emotions of crowds watching him and his colleagues leave for the war at the port of Felixstowe in August 1914:

'[People were] cheering, shouting, singing, waving their handkerchiefs . . . Some of the young girls were even pelting us with flowers . . . I turned up my head and found myself inches from a woman who was staring into my face . . . As I went by I could see that she had tears in her eyes.'

Lyn Macdonald, *1914: The Days of Hope* (Penguin, 1989)

Who started the war?

Some historians have argued that Germany started World War I in order to achieve military domination of Europe. Immanuel Geiss wrote: 'Germany was the aggressor . . . deliberately provoking Russia. This drove Russia, France and Britain . . . into a position where they could not but react against massive German ambitions.' Others have agreed that Germany played the leading part in starting the war, but because of fears for its own security. The German leaders, it is argued, feared the growing power of Russia, and decided it was best to fight in 1914, while they still had a chance of victory, rather than later, when they would lose.

Many historians, however, hold that Europe slipped into war more or less by accident, and that Germany deserves no special blame. Military historian Richard Holmes, for example, wrote that Europe's 'political and military leaders were wrestling with problems quite beyond their resources' and that the events leading up to the war were a 'calamity' that in reality no one could control.

Niall Ferguson, *The Pity of War* (Penguin, 1998); Richard Holmes, *The Western Front* (BBC, 1999)

over France before the massive but inefficient Russian army could move into action.

As soon as the Russians began to mobilize their troops, the German generals put the Schlieffen Plan into operation, even though Russia's intention was only to protect Serbia from an attack by Austria-Hungary. The kaiser contacted his cousin, Tsar Nicholas II of Russia, on 29 July, with an appeal for peace, and the tsar agreed. But General Helmuth von Moltke, head of the German general staff, argued that to stop war preparations would leave Germany exposed to a Russian invasion.

Germany declared war on Russia on 1 August, after the Russians refused to halt mobilization. Two days later, Germany declared war on France, when France refused to promise to keep out of the war. Whether Britain would enter the conflict was at that point still uncertain. Some British leaders felt that Britain must go to war in support of France and in order to maintain a 'balance of power' in Europe. They believed that if Germany managed to dominate the European mainland, this would be a threat to British independence. But others argued that Britain should stay out of a continental war. The issue was settled, however, when Germany invaded neutral Belgium on 4 August. Britain had guaranteed Belgium's neutrality and declared war on Germany in its defence.

The majority of the people in the fighting nations supported the war, and cheering, flag-waving crowds filled the centres of major cities across Europe.

CHAPTER 2

VICTORY BY CHRISTMAS?

Plans to mobilize armies were quickly implemented and by August 1914, some 6 million men were ready for war in Europe. Field Marshal Lord Horatio Herbert Kitchener, appointed British Secretary of State for War at the start of the conflict, warned the British government that the war would probably last from three to four years. But most people believed that the war would be decided quickly by a series of destructive but rapidly fought battles. The general expectation was that it would be 'all over by Christmas'.

At first, it seemed there might indeed be a quick end to the conflict. Within less than a month of the beginning of the war, Germany appeared to be on the point of victory. The Germans, pursuing the Schlieffen Plan, concentrated the major part of their forces on an offensive through Belgium. The small Belgian army fought back bravely, slowing the Germans' progress, but Germany soon broke through and advanced towards the French border. On the way, German soldiers burned down villages and towns, and executed groups of civilians suspected of acts of resistance. These atrocities turned many formerly neutral people, especially in the United States, against Germany.

Meanwhile, in mid-August, the French army began an offensive in Lorraine, intending to break through the German defences and surge into Germany itself.

August 1914 saw German soldiers marching through the Belgian capital, Brussels. The invasion sent shock waves around the world.

Fierce firepower

Charles de Gaulle, a future president of France, was a captain in the French army in 1914. He described the shock felt by French troops – brought up to believe that bravery was the key to victory in war – when they first encountered German firepower:

'Suddenly the enemy's fire became precise and concentrated. Second by second the hail of bullets and the thunder of shells grew stronger. Those who survived lay flat on the ground, amid the screaming wounded and the humble corpses . . . In an instant it had become clear that not all the courage in the world could withstand this fire.'

Richard Holmes, *The Western Front* (BBC, 1999)

The offensive was a disaster. The French infantry and cavalry were massacred by machine guns, rapid rifle fire and artillery as they launched one attack after another on the German fortified positions. The French lost hundreds of thousands of troops in this Battle of the Frontiers, and were driven back in complete disarray.

By 20 August, British troops had been shipped across the English Channel and had taken up a position on the extreme left of the French line. The British Expeditionary Force (BEF) was small by continental standards – consisting of a little over 100,000 men – because Britain did not have conscription, just a small professional army. Very soon the BEF found itself directly in the path of the far more powerful German forces as they advanced through Belgium. On 24 August, the British troops clashed with the Germans at Mons. After a valiant fight, the BEF was forced to withdraw. Throughout the rest of August, the British and their French allies retreated towards Paris in the face of the advancing German army.

While the Germans looked triumphant on the Western Front, they seemed in trouble in the east. The basis of German strategy was the hope that victory in the west could be achieved before the Russian forces could mount a serious attack on Germany. But the Russians mobilized far faster and more effectively

Members of the British Expeditionary Force (BEF) and Belgian soldiers retreat after the Battle of Mons. They were unable to hold their positions in the face of the onslaught.

After their victory at Tannenberg, German Field Marshal Paul von Hindenburg (centre), and his chief of staff, General Erich Ludendorff (right), became national heroes in Germany.

Taxis race to war

On 3 September 1914, General Joseph Galliéni, the commander of French troops in Paris, was preparing to defend the city against the advancing German First Army. Reconnaissance aircraft reported that the Germans had turned southwards to pass east of Paris. The following day, in a desperate attempt to protect the capital, Galliéni launched a bold attack on the flank of the German army near the River Marne. At one point, lacking transport, French troops were rushed from Paris to the battlefield in taxis. The surprise attack was a success and turned the tide of the war. Other Allied troops also counter-attacked and forced the Germans to retreat. Paris was saved.

than the Germans had thought possible. By 17 August, Russian armies were advancing into German territory in East Prussia. The Germans responded rapidly by appointing Field Marshal Paul von Hindenburg to command the Eastern Front, with General Erich Ludendorff as his chief of staff. They also transferred some troops from the Western Front to strengthen their forces in the east.

GERMANY VS RUSSIA

The Germans were heavily outnumbered by the Russians in East Prussia, but by skilful manoeuvring, Hindenburg and Ludendorff achieved a devastating victory at the Battle of Tannenberg on 26–31 August. Around 100,000 Russian troops were taken prisoner, and as many as 50,000 were killed or wounded. The Russian commander, General Alexander Samsonov, committed suicide. The Germans went on to drive Russian forces out of East Prussia, which ended the threat of an invasion of Germany from the east.

But Germany's ally, Austria-Hungary, was not doing so well. The first attempt by the Austro-Hungarian army to invade Serbia proved a costly failure, as the Serb troops proved more than a match for the invaders. In Galicia, the Russians were winning their battles against Austro-Hungarian forces and, in early

September, Russia captured the city of Lemberg. Germany was now forced to transfer troops from East Prussia to the south to support the Austro-Hungarians.

Meanwhile, on the Western Front, the run of German successes ended in the first week of September. According to the Schlieffen Plan, the German armies sweeping down from Belgium were supposed to advance behind the French armies facing the German border. The French would be encircled and destroyed. But the German victory in Lorraine had driven the French back from the frontier zone, making encirclement more difficult. Also, the long march through Belgium and northern France had exhausted German troops and stretched their lines of supply severely.

The Germans swung to the east of Paris, instead of to the west as originally planned, partly to reduce the distance they had to travel. As they neared the east of Paris, the French and

French soldiers using a machine gun left behind by the retreating German army during the Battle of the Marne in September 1914. The Allied troops were at a huge disadvantage at this stage of the war because they did not have enough machine guns of their own.

British counter-attacked at the Battle of the Marne. On 9 September, the German high command ordered its forces to retreat northwards. The Allies set off in pursuit, sensing that victory was close. But when the Germans reached the Aisne River, they dug trenches and were able to hold their ground.

Soldiers from Africa and Asia played an important part in World War I. Here, cavalry soldiers from Algeria are seen resting after a battle.

MILLIONS KILLED

A large area of open country between the Aisne River and the English Channel coast remained no-man's-land. From

September through to November, the Germans and the Allies edged closer to the sea as each side made a series of attempts to gain control of this area. This 'Race to the Sea' resulted in a number of extremely costly battles as each successive outflanking move was blocked. The final battle, near the Belgian town of Ypres, lasted

How close was Germany to winning the war?

The Bulgarian army prepares to move up to the front line in October 1915. Like all armies in World War I, they depended heavily on horse-drawn vehicles.

Some historians believe that the Germans could have defeated France between August and September 1914, if they had implemented the original Schlieffen Plan properly. The plan called for German military strength to focus on a quick advance down from Belgium to encircle and destroy the French. But the German commander, Field Marshal Helmuth von Moltke, weakened German forces by transferring two corps to fight Russia on the Eastern Front. Other historians have questioned, however, whether the Schlieffen Plan could ever have succeeded. It required German troops to advance on foot some 40 km (25 miles) a day and fight at the end of ever-lengthening supply lines. Under these circumstances, the exhausted Germans would have become increasingly vulnerable to a counter-attack.

from 19 October to 22 November and is estimated to have cost a quarter of a million British, French and German casualties.

From mid-November, the onset of winter brought an end to the 'war of movement'. The two sides dug themselves into trenches, facing one another along a front line that stretched unbroken from the English Channel in the north to the border of neutral Switzerland in the south. On the Eastern Front, another looser line was held as Christmas approached. The human cost of the fighting in 1914 had been unprecedented in any previous wars. France and Germany combined lost over half a million young men. Around a third of the British troops sent to France in August had died. Russia and Austria-Hungary each had well over a million soldiers who were dead, wounded or taken prisoner. Yet this fighting had not produced a decisive result.

CHAPTER 3

A LONG WAR

By the end of 1914, Germany had taken control of a valuable part of northern France, with many factories and mines, and most of Belgium. But the new year saw Britain and France determined to force the Germans out and regain all of this territory. However, their large-scale offensives made no progress. Battles such as Neuve Chapelle in March 1915 and Loos in September resulted in nothing but heavy casualties.

The front line from the English Channel to Switzerland remained unchanged throughout the year, except in minor detail.

The reason for the stalemate on the Western Front was the dominance of defence over attack. On both sides, armies dug systems of trenches to protect themselves against enemy fire. Barbed wire was set out in front of the trench. To attack, soldiers had to climb out of their trenches and cross no-man's-land, where they were fired on by rifles, machine guns and artillery. They then had to pass through the barbed wire to occupy the enemy trench. The defenders would sometimes have a second trench behind the first, so the whole process then had to be

To protect themselves from gas attacks, these French soldiers are wearing eye goggles and chemical-soaked pads over their mouths.

Deadly gas

Poison gas was first used by the Germans at Ypres in April 1915. Six days after the first gas attack, British general John Charteris wrote in his diary:

'The horrible part of it is the slow lingering death of those who are gassed. I saw some hundred poor fellows laid out in the open . . . slowly drowning with water in their lungs.'

H. P. Willmott, *World War I* (Dorling Kindersley, 2003)

Britain had to use women workers in armaments factories to supply the huge amount of weaponry needed by the military.

repeated. Even if an attacking force managed to create a gap in the enemy's defences, it lacked the mobility to advance swiftly through the hole it had made, and the defenders were able to bring up reserves to plug the gap.

It was common to use artillery bombardment to 'soften up' enemy defences before an attack, but the shells had only a limited effect against well-entrenched troops. At the Second Battle of Ypres in April 1915, the Germans used poison gas for the first time in an attempt to disrupt defences, at first with some success. Gas was soon extensively used by the Allies as well, but the development of gas masks quickly limited its effectiveness on either side. The use of chemical warfare made the battlefield even more dangerous and terrifying, but had no decisive effect.

On the Eastern Front, warfare was more mobile than in the west, because there was more room to manoeuvre in the vast spaces. During 1915,

the Russians fared badly and had to retreat when the Germans and Austro-Hungarians advanced in the summer. But even so, there was little chance of a quick decisive victory.

All sides faced the prospect of a long war, the success of which would rely on a massive increase in the production of weapons and of manpower. By the start of 1915, all the armies were already running short on munitions, especially artillery shells. Countries realized that they needed to organize their industries to maximum effect to support the war effort, while at the same time recruiting the largest possible number of men to fight. Britain held out for a long time against the need to introduce conscription. Around 2.5 million British citizens joined the army as volunteers between 1914 and 1916 – almost as many as the army could accommodate. Britain could also draw on troops from its empire and dominions. Canada, Australia, New Zealand and India in particular provided large forces of fighting men. But eventually, even in Britain, conscription was introduced in January 1916.

Civilians were rarely the direct targets of military action, although some air raids were carried out on cities as German zeppelins (airships), attacked London from 1915 onwards. But civilians were seriously affected by the war in other ways. With millions of men away fighting, women were expected to do jobs formerly done exclusively by

Soldiers from India fought bravely and suffered heavy casualties on the Western Front in 1914 and 1915.

TURNING POINTS IN HISTORY

Lusitania torpedoed

On 7 May 1915, one of the world's largest and most luxurious passenger ships, the *Lusitania*, was torpedoed by a German submarine. The ship sank in 18 minutes, drowning more than 1,200 passengers and crew. The liner had been sailing from New York to Liverpool, and 128 of the drowned passengers were Americans. The Germans claimed that the liner had been carrying troops and military equipment but, in fact, it had only a small quantity of ammunition on board. The attack caused anti-German riots in Britain, and outraged American public opinion. Shortly afterwards, fearful that the United States would join the war, Germany scaled down its U-boat activity.

men – from driving buses and working the land to working in armaments factories. There were increasing shortages of essential goods, including staple foods, which led to hunger and unrest in many European cities.

Britain and France were better placed than their enemies for a long war, because they could import supplies such as food and raw materials by sea from around the world. The United States was an especially important supplier. Germany tried to cut off these supplies by using submarines, called U-boats, to sink merchant ships bound for Britain. But the U-boat campaign had to be limited from mid-1915, after the United States threatened to enter the war and support the Allies if attacks on American ships continued.

Meanwhile, Britain used its impressive Royal Navy warships as a blockade that effectively stopped food and raw materials for industry from being imported by the Central Powers. The rival navies of Britain and Germany fought only one major sea battle, at Jutland from 31 May to 1 June 1916. Although the Royal Navy lost more ships than the Germans, the battle confirmed British domination of the sea, and the German fleet never left port again in the course of the war.

Escalation

As the war continued, more countries were drawn into the conflict. Italy joined the war on the Allied side in May 1915, after the Allies secretly

Heavy artillery, such as this Italian howitzer, was used by all sides in the war. But the tactic of heavy shelling failed to bring about a decisive breakthrough in trench warfare.

Reasons for fighting

Conditions for the average soldier during World War I were appalling and the chances of death or serious injury extremely high. So why did the men continue to fight? One obvious reason was what military historian Keith Simpson called 'fear of the consequences of disobedience'. For example, 346 British soldiers were executed for refusing to fight. There was also a strong sense of solidarity with comrades in arms – soldiers did not want to let their friends down. Patriotism was also a powerful motive – many soldiers felt it was their duty to win the war on behalf of their country. British war correspondent Philip Gibbs wrote of men on opposing sides being driven by 'a deep and simple love of England [or] Germany'.

But historian Niall Ferguson asserts that an instinctive love of fighting and killing also played its part. He wrote: 'Men kept fighting because they wanted to.' He quotes a Canadian soldier who described the war as 'the greatest adventure of my life. I would not have missed it for anything.'

Keith Simpson quoted in Richard Holmes, *The Western Front* (BBC, 1999); Philip Gibbs quoted in H. P. Willmott, *World War I* (Dorling Kindersley, 2003); Niall Ferguson, *The Pity of War* (Penguin, 1998)

agreed that the Italians could seize territory from Austria-Hungary if they achieved victory. In the summer of 1915, Bulgaria joined Germany and Austria-Hungary in an offensive in the Balkans, finally breaking Serbian resistance. Serbia was then occupied by the Central Powers and the Serbian army fled into exile.

Further afield, Japan declared war on Germany and took the opportunity to seize German possessions in China and the Pacific. Germany's colonies in Africa were attacked by troops from the British dominion of South Africa. But by far the most important development came as a result of the Ottoman Empire (Turkey) entering the war on the German side in November 1914. Because the Turks ruled an area stretching from the Mediterranean to Mesopotamia, their involvement in the war had far-reaching consequences for the entire Middle East.

Faced with stalemate on the Western Front, in the spring of 1915, Britain decided to try to capture the Ottoman capital, Constantinople (Istanbul), with the aim of opening up a sea route to provide military support to Russia. A large military force, including many Australians and New Zealanders, landed on the Turkish coast at Gallipoli in April, in order to seize control of the straits that led to Constantinople. But the troops met fierce resistance from the Turkish army, and 250,000 men were killed or wounded before the operation was finally abandoned in January 1916.

In other areas of the Ottoman Empire, the British fought the Turks with mixed success in Mesopotamia, and supported a revolt by Arabs against Turkish rule in what is now Saudi Arabia. For their part, the Turks invaded the Caucasus region of Russia in the winter of 1914–1915, only to be driven back with heavy losses. Wherever the war spread, it brought death and suffering on a terrifying and unprecedented scale.

An Australian soldier carries a wounded comrade during the fighting at Gallipoli in 1915.

CHAPTER 4

THE PRESSURE MOUNTS

By 1916, the war had grown to encompass many parts of the world outside Europe. However, the combatant countries remained convinced that it was on the battlefields of Europe that the conflict would be won or lost. After the frustrations of 1915, military leaders prepared for even greater offensives in 1916, and readied themselves to use the now huge quantity of arms and ammunition being supplied by their war factories.

In December 1915, a conference had been held at Chantilly, France. Here the British, French, Italians and Russians had agreed on a plan to attack the Central Powers simultaneously so they would have to fight on all fronts at once. But the Germans had their own attack plans. General Erich von Falkenhayn, who had taken over from Moltke as German chief of general staff, decided to concentrate his forces against the French fortress city of Verdun. He believed that the French would feel obliged to defend Verdun whatever the cost. Falkenhayn wrote that it would become a killing ground on which 'the forces of France will bleed to death'.

The Germans launched their offensive against Verdun on 21 February 1916, with the heaviest artillery bombardment the world had yet seen. As Falkenhayn had guessed, the French government decreed that Verdun must be held at whatever cost. General Philippe Pétain was put in command of the city's defence, and hundreds of thousands of French troops were sent into that small sector of the front. The only route for supplies was a single road, soon known to the French as the *voie sacrée* (sacred way). Around 3,000 trucks travelled along it every day, carrying men and supplies to the battlefield, despite the fact that it was under continual artillery bombardment.

Falkenhayn had hoped that the French troops would soon be worn down by artillery fire, and that he could keep German casualties low. But the German troops were increasingly drawn into fierce combat, some of it at close quarters in and around the old forts that had been built to defend Verdun.

VOICES FROM HISTORY

Horror of war

German soldiers suffered as heavily as the British and French in the battles of 1916. Lieutenant Ernst Jünger described the German lines in September 1916:

'The sunken road now appeared as nothing but a series of enormous shell-holes filled with pieces of uniform, weapons and dead bodies . . . Among the living lay the dead. As we dug ourselves in we found them in layers stacked one on top of the other. One company after another had been shoved into the drum-fire [machine-gun fire] and steadily annihilated.'

Ernst Jünger, *Storm of Steel* (Penguin, 2004)

French soldiers crouch down as artillery shells explode around them during the Battle of Verdun in 1916. On the first day of the battle, German guns fired over a million shells to try to break French resistance.

By the time the offensive was called off in early June, the Germans had suffered over 280,000 casualties – a number only slightly smaller than the 315,000 French dead or wounded. Worse still for Germany, despite their fierce offensive, they failed to take Verdun and France claimed a victory.

At the Chantilly conference, the British and French had agreed to launch a joint offensive on the section of the Western Front near the Somme River in the summer of 1916. The huge French losses at Verdun meant that the French army had only limited resources left to throw into a new offensive. The British army, however, had been growing rapidly as volunteers joined up in the hundreds of thousands. So the Somme offensive became a largely British operation, under the command of Field Marshal Sir Douglas Haig.

Haig believed that a prolonged artillery bombardment, backed up by the exploding of mines in tunnels dug under the German lines, would break German resistance. The infantry would then advance to occupy the wrecked German trenches and the cavalry would ride through into open country behind the German lines. But the first day of the battle, 1 July, was a disaster and proved that the artillery was nowhere near as effective as Haig expected. The following months reinforced this lesson. Despite attack after attack by Allied infantry, the German lines barely moved. Beaumont-Hamel, for example, was one of the objectives that the British intended to seize on 1 July; they actually took it on 13 November, the day the offensive was finally called off.

Around 600,000 Allied troops were killed or wounded in the Battle of the Somme. Estimates of German casualties vary, but they were almost certainly on a similar scale. Overshadowed by this immense slaughter were a few positive developments. Britain's new volunteer army was beginning to learn how to fight – a painful and expensive learning process. Also, new weapons

British soldiers wearing gas masks man a machine gun during the Battle of the Somme in 1916.

The Somme

On 1 July 1916, the British army, together with a smaller number of French troops, launched a major offensive on the Somme. Eight days before the attack, over a million artillery shells were fired at the German trenches. This bombardment was expected to crush German resistance. British infantry – comprised mostly of new troops fighting their first battle – were ordered to advance at walking pace across no-man's-land to occupy the German lines. But as the troops advanced, the Germans emerged unscathed from their deep shelters and opened fire. The shelling had also failed to clear away the barbed wire in front of the German trenches. Unable to advance, and caught in machine-gun fire, line after line of British soldiers were mowed down. Of the 100,000 men who attacked that day, almost 20,000 were killed and another 40,000 were wounded or missing in action.

were introduced that could potentially break the deadlock. The British used tanks for the first time at the Somme, although there were very few of them, and they were too slow and unreliable to have much effect in this battle. Also,

aircraft had begun to play an important part in the war – used mainly as 'eyes in the sky' to direct artillery fire on to enemy targets. But the planes were not yet very effective as bombers, or for attacking troops on the ground. For the time being, increasing supplies of arms and munitions simply increased the number of dead and wounded.

HUGE LOSSES

During 1916, there was more movement on the Eastern Front than in the west, but this still resulted in mass slaughter on a similar scale. In the spring, the Russians launched an offensive in Poland. Their troops outnumbered the Germans by six to one, yet the Russians were driven back with heavy losses. In June, however, Russian general Alexei Brusilov launched a successful offensive against Austro-Hungarian forces in Galicia. His troops attacked without any initial artillery bombardment and took the Austro-Hungarians by surprise. Their soldiers retreated in disarray and the Russians took more than 300,000 prisoners. In the face of such losses, Germany was forced to transfer troops from the Western Front in order to counter-attack the Russians. However, despite the initial success, Russia lost around a million men in the Brusilov offensive – killed, wounded or taken prisoner – for little real gain.

Battered by the Russian offensive and also fighting the Italians in the south, by the summer of 1916 the Austro-Hungarian army was almost on its knees. Germany had to take over command of its ally's military forces to keep them fighting. This move proved very effective when the Romanian government declared war on the Central Powers in August 1916. Romania hoped to take advantage of Austria-Hungary's weakness to seize territory from Hungary. But Romania was soon invaded by armies under German command, and its capital, Bucharest, fell to the Central Powers in December.

With the huge losses at the front and no prospect of an end to the war in sight, people's support for their governments was stretched almost to breaking point. Civilians in many warring countries faced serious food shortages and other problems, especially in Austria-Hungary and Russia. In Austria-Hungary, the loyalty of the different nationalities within the empire weakened as the war

David Lloyd George (right), British prime minister from December 1916, talks to French commander, General Joseph Joffre (centre) and British commander, Field Marshal Sir Douglas Haig.

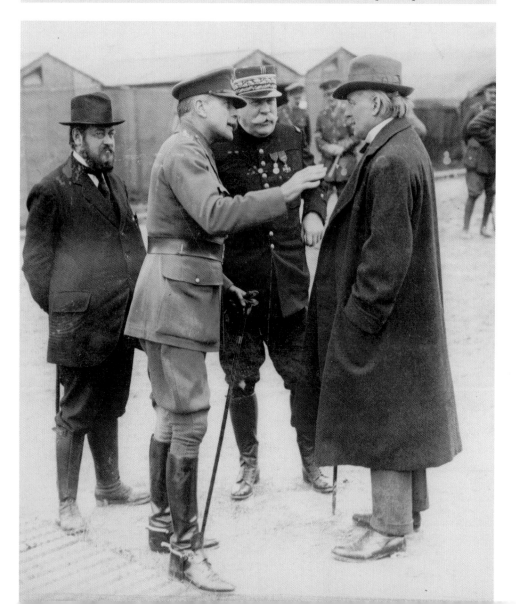

Lions led by donkeys?

The soldiers in the trenches have been described as 'lions led by donkeys' – courageous men who were sent to their deaths in futile offensives ordered by generals who were incompetent fools. Historian A. J. P. Taylor summed up this view of the war as: 'brave helpless soldiers; blundering obstinate generals; nothing achieved'.

But other historians have argued that the generals fought the war in the only way that it could be fought, at a time when artillery, machine guns and barbed wire dominated the battlefield. Historian John Keegan wrote: 'The basic and stark fact . . . was that the conditions of warfare between 1914 and 1918 predisposed towards slaughter and that only an entirely different technology, one not available until a generation later, could have averted such an outcome.'

A. J. P. Taylor, *The First World War* (Penguin, 1963); John Keegan, *The First World War* (Hutchinson, 1998)

continued. There were, for example, large-scale desertions by Czech troops from the Austro-Hungarian army during 1916. Britain faced its own nationalist problem in Ireland, where Republicans seeking independence from British rule staged an uprising in Dublin in Easter 1916, hoping for German support that never came. The uprising was repressed by the British army in a brutal manner that turned many more Irish people against British rule. Meanwhile in Russia, the tsarist regime had driven the poor and poverty-stricken to the brink of a revolution by the end of 1916. That revolution would change the course of world history.

General Alexei Brusilov was the most successful Russian general of the war. His offensive in the summer of 1916 was a severe setback for Austria-Hungary. But ultimately, his offensive cost Russia many men without any decisive victory.

CHAPTER 5

AMERICA DECLARES WAR

French soldiers make their way towards German lines to surrender to the enemy. In April–May 1917, after a disastrous offensive, many French soldiers refused to obey orders and organized protests.

After nearly two and a half years of huge losses, dreadful casualties, and very little strategic success, the Central Powers were ready to make a deal with the Allies. At the end of 1916, the German government made an offer of peace to the Allies. But part of their offer was that Germany should keep possession of the territory it currently held – a proposal totally unacceptable to the Allied powers. The peace offer was rejected, so German leaders decided upon a desperate gamble. They would resume unlimited U-boat warfare, hoping to sink enough merchant ships carrying supplies to Britain from America to bring Britain to its knees. The Germans knew that the United States would probably enter the war if its merchant ships were sunk, but gambled that the war could be won before American manpower and industrial might could have any real effect on the European battlefields.

Confident that the U-boats could win the war, the Germans decided to adopt a defensive strategy and regroup their soldiers on the Western Front. In early 1917, German troops were withdrawn to newly constructed fortified positions along what was known as the Hindenburg Line. The French army was now under the command of Robert Nivelle, who replaced Joseph Joffre as French commander-in-chief, and who promised to 'win the war in 48 hours' with a single, concentrated offensive. Launched in April 1917, the

Nivelle Offensive was an utter disaster. The Allies lost around 350,000 men for almost no gain. In the wake of the offensive, there were widespread mutinies in the French army. Nivelle was dismissed and replaced by General Pétain, who restored order in the ranks with a mixture of firmness and concessions. But the spirit of the French army was broken.

Allied offensives on the Western Front, with British and Commonwealth forces playing the leading role, continued through 1917. The fighting at Ypres in July through to November, which became known as the Battle of Passchendaele, was some of the worst

Thousands of French soldiers, captured by the Germans during the Nivelle offensive of spring 1917, are taken away to a prisoner-of-war camp.

VOICES FROM HISTORY

An end to war

Siegfried Sassoon was a British poet and army officer with a record of exceptional bravery. In 1917, he felt that the war must be ended. He issued a public appeal for peace:

'I believe that the war is being deliberately prolonged by those who have the power to end it . . . I have seen and endured the suffering of the troops, and I can no longer be a party to prolong these sufferings for ends which I believe to be evil and unjust.'

Sassoon's plea for peace was dismissed by the authorities as the product of shell shock, and he was sent to a military hospital.

Jon Stallworthy, *Wilfred Owen: A Biography* (OUP, 1975)

Shell holes are used by Canadian soldiers to provide cover during the fighting at Passchendaele in 1917. The continuous shelling and heavy rain created deep, treacherous mud.

of the entire war. Constant rainfall reduced the battlefield to a swamp and many soldiers drowned in the mud. As usual, Allied advances of a few hundred metres cost tens of thousands of casualties. Meanwhile, in Italy, German and Austro-Hungarian forces managed a breakthrough at Caporetto in October. This forced Britain and France to transfer resources to the Italian front to prevent their ally from being defeated.

REVOLUTION IN RUSSIA

In 1917, there was stalemate on the Western Front, but on the Eastern Front dramatic changes were about to alter the course of the war. In Russia, hunger and grinding poverty were creating increased resentment towards the wealthy tsarist regime. In March, Tsar Nicholas II was forced to abdicate after an uprising provoked by food shortages in the capital, Petrograd (St Petersburg). A provisional government took over, with plans to continue the war. The strongest figure in the new government was Alexander Kerensky. In the summer of 1917, Kerensky ordered a major offensive to drive the enemy from Russian soil. It proved a costly failure.

Meanwhile, anti-war feeling in Russia was mounting. Russian revolutionary Vladimir Ilyich Lenin, the leader of the Bolshevik Party, was in exile in Switzerland when the tsarist regime

The Zimmermann telegram

On 17 January 1917, the German foreign minister, Arthur Zimmermann, sent the German ambassador in Mexico a proposal for a military alliance between Germany and Mexico. The telegram suggested that with German support, the Mexicans 'reconquer the lost territory in Texas, New Mexico and Arizona' from the United States. Zimmermann did not know that both British and American intelligence services were monitoring transatlantic communications, and they intercepted the message. In early March, the content of the telegram was revealed to the American public. They were outraged, and American opinion turned decisively against Germany.

their officers. The Bolsheviks overthrew Kerensky's provisional government in 1917 and set up their own revolutionary government with Lenin at its head. Lenin immediately issued a proclamation calling on the people in all combatant countries to revolt against their rulers and end the war. On 15 December, the Bolsheviks signed an armistice with the Germans and opened peace negotiations.

The collapse of Russia was a great boost for the Germans. It was a triumph that they desperately needed, because by this time the resumption of U-boat attacks in February 1917 had finally pushed the United States to the brink of entering the war.

Vladimir Ilyich Lenin, the leader of the revolutionary Bolshevik party, addresses a crowd in Petrograd (St Petersburg) during the Russian Revolution.

fell. In April, Lenin accepted a German offer of transport back to his homeland. As the Germans had hoped, once back in Russia, Lenin demanded an immediate end to the war and a further, more extreme, revolution. His slogan was: 'Bread, Peace and Land'.

After the failure of the Kerensky offensive, the Russian army began to fall apart. Soldiers deserted in the thousands, or formed revolutionary committees and ignored orders from

In March 1918, Germany and its allies met representatives of the Russian government at Brest-Litovsk to sign an armistice.

US President Woodrow Wilson saw himself as a man of peace. He had been narrowly re-elected in 1916 with the slogan: 'He kept us out of the war.' But, on 2 April, he asked Congress to authorize a declaration of war on Germany, saying: 'The world must be made safe for democracy.' America entered the war on 6 April, but tried to keep its distance from Britain and France. Instead of joining the Allies formally, the United States became only an 'Associate Power'.

STOPPING THE U-BOATS

In April 1917, one in four ships sailing to Britain was sunk and Britain was not receiving the imports it needed to survive. American troops could never be shipped across to Europe if boats were being destroyed on such a scale. But in May, Britain introduced a convoy system. Merchant ships crossed the Atlantic in large groups under naval protection. The result was a drop in losses from around 25 per cent to 1 per cent. This meant that Britain could go on fighting.

The United States had only a small army. Training and equipping a large force to fight in Europe was a slow process, so the Americans had no immediate impact on the fighting. But the entry of the United States into the war and the fall of the tsar in Russia together had a profound effect on war aims. The Allies were now able to present their war as a struggle for

What were America's reasons for declaring war?

US President Woodrow Wilson stated that America entered World War I as 'the champion of right and liberty'. He claimed that the United States had no selfish motive – not even 'to defend our territory'.

This idealistic view of American action has been disputed by some historians who argue that the United States took advantage of the war to increase its economic and political power. They believe that selling supplies to Britain and France had become vital to the American economy. Americans had also lent the Allies very large sums of money to pay for these supplies. If the Allies lost the war, they would be unable to repay these huge debts and the US economy would suffer, so America had to ensure that the Allies did not lose.

Other historians have argued that German domination of Europe would have been a long-term threat to American security and therefore had to be stopped. However, there is no documentary evidence to show that President Wilson had any other than idealistic motives.

American soldiers say goodbye to family and friends as they set off on the long journey to Europe. More than 2 million US servicemen crossed the Atlantic.

democracy, freedom and the right of national groups to govern themselves. This had not been possible while the Russian tsarist regime – an enemy of democracy – was an ally.

The changing situation also encouraged anti-war feeling in Germany. For many Germans, the main motive for supporting the war had been fear of conquest by tsarist Russia. With the threat of the tsar gone, in July 1917, the German Reichstag (parliament) voted in favour of a 'peace resolution'. But the Reichstag did not have control over the German high command. Encouraged by the collapse of Russia, in November 1917, Ludendorff and his colleagues decided that, in the following spring, they would launch a final colossal offensive on the Western Front that could win the war for the Central Powers.

CHAPTER 6

END OF THE STALEMATE

On 3 March 1918, several German representatives met with members of the Russian Bolshevik government at Brest-Litovsk to sign a peace treaty. It was a humiliating agreement for the Bolsheviks, but they had no choice. The Russian army had dissolved and Russia was at the mercy of German military power. The peace agreement forced Russia to accept a loss of nearly a third of the population of the former Russian Empire: Poland, Ukraine, Belarus, Finland, Moldova, Armenia, Azerbaijan, Georgia, and the Baltic states of Lithuania, Latvia and Estonia all became independent, at least in principle. In practice, they were now under the strict control and ruthless economic exploitation of Germany and the Austro-Hungarian Empire.

The harsh peace settlement imposed on Russia convinced even many

British soldiers killed during the German offensive of spring 1918.

American soldiers fight on the Western Front. Germany's new offensives in 1918 caused heavy casualties for Britain and France, but they were made up by the arrival of the Americans.

As early as 23 March 1918, Kaiser Wilhelm granted all German schoolchildren a holiday to celebrate 'Victory Day'. But he acted too soon. The Allies rallied despite the overwhelming onslaught and for the first time in the war, British and French forces were joined under a single commander in chief, French general Ferdinand Foch. Despite their gains of territory, the Germans suffered heavy losses – 348,000 in the first six weeks of the offensive. The Allies also lost hundreds of thousands of men, but enough American 'doughboys' – the nickname for the American infantrymen – were arriving in Europe to replace them. About 200,000 US troops landed in France in the month of May alone. Commanded by General John Pershing, they fought their first action against the Germans at Château-Thierry on the Marne in early June.

Germans that Germany's rulers were fighting a war of conquest, not of self-defence. There was a wave of strikes in German and Austro-Hungarian factories by workers who sympathized with the Bolsheviks and who demanded peace terms that were fair.

Germany's military leaders knew that American soldiers would begin to arrive in Europe very soon and that they must take advantage of their triumph in the east before this happened. They decided to transfer troops from Russia to reinforce the Western Front. So, on 21 March 1918, masses of German troops supported by over 10,000 artillery guns and mortars were deployed to launch an offensive against the British armies on the Somme. Known as the Michael Offensive or the *Kaiserschlacht* (kaiser's battle), it was, to begin with, an overwhelming success. The British lines were torn apart, bringing to an end the long stalemate on the Western Front. Follow-up offensives in April and May took the Germans to within less than 105 km (65 miles) of Paris.

VOICES FROM HISTORY

Rallying the troops

British military leaders feared that their army might be facing defeat in April 1918. The British commander, Field Marshal Douglas Haig, issued a ringing proclamation to rally his troops, who were bearing the weight of the German offensive:

'With our backs to the wall and believing in the justice of our cause, each one of us must fight to the end . . . Every position must be held to the last man.'

Quoted in John Keegan, *The First World War* (Hutchinson 1998)

French tanks advance towards the front in 1918. The large-scale use of tanks by the Allies in 1918 helped to break the crippling stalemate.

The Germans continued to attack through the early summer, but with less and less success. By August, the Allies were ready to launch a counter-offensive. On 8 August, Canadian and Australian infantry, supported by 350 tanks and over 2,000 aircraft, attacked the Germans at Amiens. Ludendorff called it 'the black day of the German army'. German troops were pushed back and suffered heavy casualties. Two days later, Ludendorff told the kaiser that Germany could no longer hope to win the war.

The Allies launched a series of successful offensives throughout the following months. By early October, they had crossed the Hindenburg Line into territory the Germans had held since 1914. The Allies were far superior to the Germans in the use of tanks, which were now a major force on the battlefield, and Allied planes dominated the air, bombing and strafing German soldiers and supply lines. The support of the newly arrived American troops also helped – their freshness boosted morale and energy, although their inexperience meant they often suffered heavy casualties. The Germans, however, were worn down by years of fighting and demoralized by the failure of their spring offensive. They began to surrender in increasing numbers.

TURNING POINTS IN HISTORY

A plan for peace

On 8 January 1918, President Wilson presented a fourteen-point plan for peace to the US Congress. Some of the points were general proposals for a better, more peaceful world after the war. For example, a reduction of all countries' armaments to the minimum required for national defence, and the establishment of an international organization to guarantee countries had protection from attack by their neighbours. Other points were more specific. Germany was to hand back territory occupied during the war, as well as Alsace-Lorraine. Poland – previously divided up between Germany, Austria-Hungary and Russia – was to become an independent state. National groups in the Austro-Hungarian and Ottoman empires were to be given a large say in running their own affairs. The existence of Wilson's peace plan became a major factor in ending the war in the autumn of 1918.

General John Pershing (left), the commander of American forces in Europe, did not agree with US President Wilson's desire for a compromise peace. Instead, he wanted total military victory.

VICTORY IN SIGHT

The Allies were having success in other parts of the world as well. In the Ottoman Empire, the British captured Jerusalem in December 1917 and defeated Turkish forces at the Battle of Megiddo in September 1918. On the Italian front, the Austro-Hungarian army was in chaos after a last failed offensive in the summer of 1918. In the Balkans, an Allied army, advancing north from the Greek port of Salonika, attacked Bulgaria on 15 September. Within two weeks, the Bulgarians had surrendered.

On 29 September, Ludendorff told the kaiser that Germany must seek an immediate end to the fighting. There were, as yet, no foreign troops

In December 1917, British troops occupied Jerusalem, which had until then been ruled by the Turks as part of the Ottoman Empire.

on German soil, and the German line on the Western Front was unbroken. In an attempt to save some national pride, the German leaders hoped to negotiate a deal that would enable them to claim to be undefeated. On 4 October, they told President Wilson that they accepted his fourteen-point peace plan, and asked him to arrange a cease-fire.

In bypassing the British and French and dealing directly with Wilson, the Germans hoped to get lenient terms. But American military leaders felt as strongly as the British and French that an armistice should have tough conditions designed to ensure that the Germans could not start another war at a later date. The conditions included the stipulation that German territory west of the Rhine was to be occupied by Allied forces, and that large quantities of German military equipment should be surrendered to the Allies. Ludendorff and other German military

WHY DID IT HAPPEN ?

Why did Germany lose?

There are a number of theories as to why the Germans lost the war. Many British military historians believe that the war was won because the British army learned to use infantry, artillery, tanks and planes in a combined, modern style of warfare that was simply too good for the Germans. Other historians have highlighted the overwhelming importance of the arrival of hundreds of thousands of fresh American troops in the summer of 1918. This contributed to what historian Niall Ferguson called 'a crisis of German morale', which saw around 360,000 German soldiers surrender in the last three months of the war.

Conversely, after the war, many Germans believed that their army had never been defeated on the battlefield. Ludendorff in particular claimed that the German army had been 'stabbed in the back' by politically motivated groups at home who undermined the war effort. But historian A. J. P. Taylor countered that losing the war caused a revolution, not the other way around: 'The German revolution was caused by Ludendorff's confession that the war was lost.'

Niall Ferguson, *The Pity of War* (Penguin, 1998); A. J. P. Taylor, *The First World War* (Penguin, 1963)

leaders considered these conditions unacceptable and wanted to fight on. But the kaiser dismissed Ludendorff on 26 October.

In reality, the worsening political situation inside Germany made continuing the war an impossible option. The German people were suffering serious hardship. The successful British naval blockade resulted in chronic shortages of food and fuel. The country was also seething with unrest. When, outraged by the armistice terms, naval commander Admiral Reinhard Scheer ordered the German fleet to set sail for a final showdown with the Royal Navy, the sailors refused to obey. Instead, the port of Kiel was taken over by protesting sailors and workers. In early November, major cities across Germany fell under revolutionary control.

In Austria-Hungary, conditions were even worse. As well as general dissatisfaction with the war, there was a lot of unrest among the different ethnic groups. The Allies encouraged the country's Poles, Czechs and other Slav minorities to organize their own governments and claim areas of Austro-Hungarian territory as their own. By the time Austria-Hungary signed the armistice on 3 November, its empire had already effectively ceased to exist.

The end of the war was in sight. On 9 November 1918, the kaiser abdicated, fleeing Germany to exile in the Netherlands. Two days later, a German delegation signed the armistice in a railway carriage in the Forest of Compiègne in eastern France. The guns fell silent on the Western Front at eleven o'clock on 11 November 1918. The war was over.

Recently captured German prisoners of war at Abbeville, France, in August 1918.

CHAPTER 7

A MIXED VICTORY

The end of the war received a mixed response. In countries on the winning side, thousands took to the streets when the armistice was announced on 11 November 1918. Delirious crowds filled major cities such as London, Paris, New York, Chicago and Melbourne. But among the victors were millions of people in no mood to celebrate – especially those who had lost brothers, sons, fathers or husbands in the war. In defeated and devastated countries around the world, there was no cause for any rejoicing at all.

No one knows for certain how many people died during World War I. The total number of men that were killed in the fighting is estimated at between 8.5 million and 9.8 million. Germany lost over 2 million men on the battlefields,

Russia probably around 1.8 million, France 1.4 million, Austria-Hungary over a million, Britain and its empire around 900,000, Italy almost half a million and the United States 50,000. Those who died in battle were mostly young men. Of German men between the ages of 19 and 22 when the war started, one in three died.

Civilians also suffered heavy casualties. For example, 700,000 German civilians may have died through hardship and malnutrition during the war and in its aftermath, mostly as a result of the British naval blockade that was maintained until June 1919.

The boulevards of Paris are flooded with people celebrating the armistice that was announced on 11 November 1918.

People visit Brookwood Cemetery in Surrey, southern England, on a memorial day in June 1919. At Brookwood, the graves of US soldiers were marked with American flags.

VOICES FROM HISTORY

Never to return

The author Vera Brittain felt a mixed reaction to the victory celebrations. She had served as a nurse during the war and had lost some of her closest friends and family. On the evening that peace was declared, she went out with some colleagues to join cheering crowds in central London. She later wrote:

'Wherever we went a burst of enthusiastic cheering greeted our Red Cross uniform, and complete strangers . . . rushed up and shook me warmly by the hand . . . I detached myself from the others and walked slowly up Whitehall, with my heart sinking in a sudden cold dismay . . . The war was over; a new age was beginning; but the dead were dead and would never return.'

Vera Brittain, *Testament of Youth* (Virago, 1978)

One unexpected and devastating by-product of the war was Spanish flu. This virulent influenza epidemic probably first appeared on the Western Front in the spring of 1918. It spread worldwide during 1918–1919, killing some 20 million people.

A NEW ORDER

In January 1919, the leaders of the victorious powers gathered in Paris for a peace conference. The defeated nations were not invited. Proceedings were dominated by the 'Big Four': Britain, France, the United States and Italy. US president Wilson wanted to create a new order in Europe based on democracy and self-determination – with borders

Diplomats watch as the peace treaty with Germany is signed on 28 June 1919.

redrawn so that each ethnic group could live under its own national government. Other leaders had different priorities. The French prime minister, Georges Clemenceau, wanted above all to weaken Germany so that it could never attack France again in the future.

A series of peace treaties were signed by the defeated countries, but the most important was the Treaty of Versailles signed by Germany. Under its terms, the Germans had to hand back Alsace-Lorraine to France, as well as give up a modest amount of other territory; for example, they had to give Poland access to the sea by a corridor across German territory to the port of Danzig (Gdansk). The German army was limited to 100,000 men, and was not allowed to possess tanks or aircraft.

The Germans were to pay 'reparations' to Britain, France, Italy and Belgium to compensate for the damage these countries had suffered. The Germans also had to admit that the war had been a result of German aggression, known as the 'war guilt clause'. Germany reluctantly signed the peace treaty on 28 June 1919 in Versailles, France, after the Allies had threatened to resume the war and invade Germany.

A French gunboat on the Ruhr River during the occupation of part of Germany in 1923.

VOICES FROM HISTORY

A display of defiance

In April 1939, German dictator Adolf Hitler described how his political career had been dedicated to undoing the Versailles Treaty:

'I have . . . endeavoured to destroy sheet by sheet the treaty which . . . contains the vilest oppression which peoples and human beings have ever been expected to put up with.'

J. Fest, *Hitler* (Weidenfeld & Nicholson, 1973)

Despite the treaties, the peacemakers had little control over what happened after the war. In the devastated Russian, Austro-Hungarian and Ottoman Empires, competing groups fought to establish not only new borders and governments, but also new states, including Finland, Poland, Czechoslovakia and Yugoslavia. The borders of the new states were mostly decided by local wars.

Inside Russia, civil war raged between the Bolshevik government and its enemies from 1918 to 1920. Eventually, the Bolsheviks took control of the majority of the territory of the former Russian Empire, which became the Soviet Union in 1922. There was also warfare in Turkey, where nationalist leader Kemal Ataturk deposed the Ottoman sultan to establish a Turkish republic, and defeated an attempt by Greece to take a large slice of Turkish territory. Britain and France reorganized the rest of the former Ottoman Empire (including the creation of the new Arab state of Iraq by the British).

The outcomes of the peace treaties and of the post-war conflicts did not fulfill Wilson's concept of self-determination. For example, Austria was forbidden to unite with Germany, even though its population was overwhelmingly German. Although Wilson's idea for an international organization to maintain peace in the future was adopted, it had limited success. The League of Nations was created to ensure that all countries would unite against any state that threatened war. But when Wilson went back to the United States after the conference, the US Congress refused to ratify the peace treaty, arguing that belonging to the League of Nations might involve America in future European wars. This

The first meeting of the new peacekeeping organization, the League of Nations, in 1920.

43

weakened the organization from the outset.

SEEDS OF DISCONTENT

At the end of World War I, many people around the world felt angry and bitter. When Germany failed to make the reparation payments laid out in the Treaty of Versailles, the Ruhr district of Germany was occupied by France and Belgium for two years from 1923, an action which plagued international relations in Europe. Around the world, countries plunged into economic instability that led to the Great Depression in the late 1920s. Mass unemployment, useless currencies and poverty were the legacy of the war for many nations – especially Germany, which had the added burden of paying both reparation and post-war debts.

The Versailles Treaty left Germany feeling wronged and humiliated. Right-wing German nationalists, such as Nazi Party leader Adolf Hitler, blamed most of their country's misfortunes on the terms of the treaty. After Hitler came to power in Germany in 1933, he was determined to restore national pride. He embarked on a policy of armed expansion that led to World War II in 1939.

Many hoped that World War I would be the 'war to end wars', but ultimately it led to another catastrophic world conflict. But it did change people's

By 1923, the countries of Europe had settled into a new shape. Germany lost territory, mostly to Poland and France. East Prussia was cut off from the rest of Germany by a strip of territory giving Poland access to the sea. The break-up of the Austro-Hungarian Empire left Austria as a small country with a mostly German population.

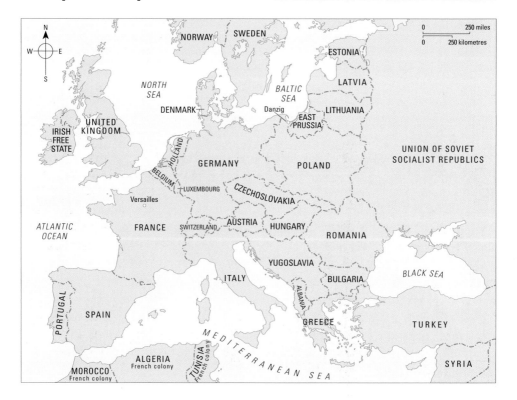

Too harsh a treaty?

Many historians believe the terms and conditions of the Treaty of Versailles were unnecessarily harsh. The German delegates who reluctantly signed the treaty in 1919 protested at 'the unheard of injustice of the conditions of peace'. Influential British economist J. M. Keynes, in his 1919 book *The Economic Consequences of the Peace*, wrote: 'The Peace [Treaty] is outrageous and impossible and can bring nothing but misfortune.'

According to historian Niall Ferguson, however, the peace terms were not especially harsh and 'Germany came out of the war no worse off than Britain, and in some respects better off.'

A large number of historians have felt that the treaty, although far from perfect, was probably the best that could have been achieved under the circumstances of the time. A. J. P. Taylor, for example, pointed out that the way the Germans were treated was inevitable, writing: 'A peace of reconciliation' would have meant accepting 'that there was nothing to choose between the two sides and that the only fault of the Germans was to have lost. Who dared say that at the time? Who, outside Germany, would say it now?'

German quote from Martin Gilbert, *A History of the Twentieth Century* (HarperCollins, 1997); J. M. Keynes quoted in Niall Ferguson, *The Pity of War* (Penguin, 1998); A. J. P. Taylor, *The First World War* (Penguin, 1963)

attitudes towards war. When World War II began, there were no cheering crowds to be seen in European cities, not even in Nazi Germany. The sacrifice of the millions who died on the Western Front and the horrors of World War I were not forgotten. This unbelievable tragedy is still remembered in annual ceremonies around the world today.

Adolf Hitler, the leader of Germany's Nazi Party, came to power in 1933. He was determined to reverse the result of World War I. This led to an even more devastating conflict in 1939–1945.

45

WORLD WAR I TIMELINE

1914

28 June: Assassination of Austrian archduke Franz Ferdinand

July: Austria-Hungary declares war on Serbia

1 August: Germany declares war on Russia

3 August: Germany declares war on France

4 August: Britain declares war on Germany

23 August: British encounter German forces at Mons

26–30 August: Battle of Tannenberg

6 September: Beginning of the First Battle of the Marne

16 November: The Ottoman Empire enters the war on the side of the Central Powers

22 November: The First Battle of Ypres ends in stalemate

1915

25 April: Allied forces land at Gallipoli, Turkey

7 May: The *Lusitania* is sunk by a German U-boat

23 May: Italy enters the war on the Allied side

July to August: Russian forces withdraw from Poland

October: Bulgaria allies itself with Central Powers

October to November: Central Powers occupy Serbia

19 December: Allied troops begin evacuation from Gallipoli

1916

21 February: The Germans launch a massive offensive against the French at Verdun

May 31: Battle of Jutland

June to July: The Brusilov offensive

June: Arabs revolt against Ottoman rule

July 1: Beginning of the Battle of the Somme

August to December: Romania enters the war and is swiftly defeated by the Central Powers

1917

February: Germany begins an unrestricted U-boat campaign

March: Collapse of the tsarist regime in Russia

6 April: The United States declares war on Germany

16 April: The start of the Nivelle Offensive

July: A final Russian offensive in Galicia fails; the Russian army begins to disintegrate

31 July to 6 November: The Third Battle of Ypres, or Battle of Passchendaele

October to December: The Caporetto Offensive, fought by German and Austrian troops against Italy

7 November: The Bolsheviks seize power in Russia

15 December: Russia and Germany agree to an armistice

1918

8 January: US President Wilson announces his 14-point peace plan

3 March: The Treaty of Brest-Litovsk

21 March: The Germans launch a massive spring offensive on the Western Front, driving the Allies back towards Paris

3 June: Battle of Château-Thierry

18 July: The Second Battle of the Marne

8 August: An Allied offensive begins at Amiens

19 September: Battle of Megiddo

30 September: Bulgaria signs an armistice with the Allies

28 October: Mutiny by German sailors at Kiel triggers revolutionary uprisings across Germany

30 October: The Ottoman Empire signs an armistice with the Allies

3 November: Austria-Hungary signs an armistice

9 November: Germany is declared a Republic and the kaiser flees into exile

11 November: Germany signs an armistice; fighting stops on the Western Front

1919

28 June: The signing of the Treaty of Versailles

GLOSSARY

abdicate To step down from a throne, giving up the right to rule a country.

Allies Term used for Britain, France and the other countries fighting on their side during the war.

annex To take over territory.

armistice An agreement between two sides in a war to stop fighting so they can negotiate a peace treaty.

assassination The murder of a public figure, usually for a political motive.

atrocities Massacres or other acts of extreme brutality.

autonomy A degree of self-government falling short of full independence.

Central Powers Term used for Germany, Austria-Hungary and their allies.

coalition government A government in which several parties co-operate.

Commonwealth An international association consisting of the UK together with states that were part of the British empire, and dependencies.

conscription Compulsory service in the armed forces.

dominion A self-governing country in the British Empire.

Great Depression Period of widespread economic failure from the late 1920s through to the 1930s, marked by high unemployment and declining trade.

merchant ship A ship carrying cargo or passengers – not a warship.

munitions Ammunition and other equipment needed by an army.

no-man's-land The area between the front line of two armies, for example between the opposing trenches on the Western Front.

Ottoman Empire A Turkish-ruled empire that controlled much of the Middle East.

outflank To advance around the side of an enemy position.

ratify To approve something formally.

reparations Payments demanded from a defeated country by the victors to compensate for damage the victors suffered in war.

self-determination The principle that people should be ruled by their choice of government.

shell shock Psychological disturbance caused by prolonged exposure to bombardment.

strafing To fire on troops on the ground from an aircraft.

FURTHER INFORMATION

Books:

The First World War: A Very Short Introduction by Michael Howard (OUP Oxford, 2007)

Tommy: The British Soldier on the Western Front by Richard Holmes (Harper Perennial, 2005)

The Western Front by Richard Holmes (BBC Books, 2008)

World War I by H.P. Willmott (Dorling Kindersley, 2003)

Websites:

Channel 4—History (www.channel4.com/programmes/tags/history)

First World War.com (www.firstworldwar.com)

PBS: The Great War (www.pbs.org/greatwar)

World War I: Trenches on the Web (www.worldwar1.com)

INDEX

Numbers in **bold** refer to pictures